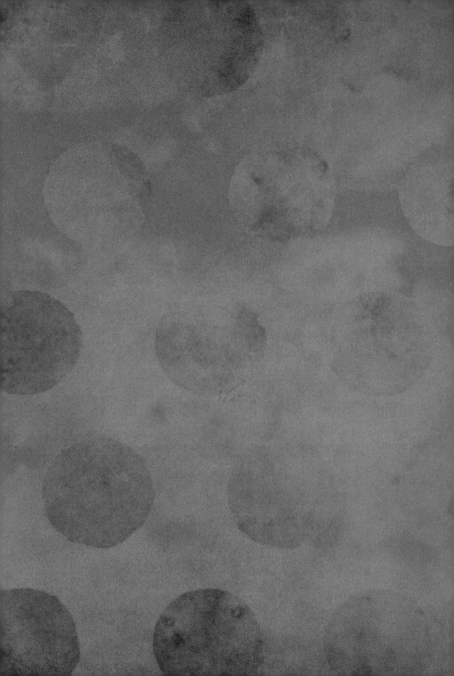

To

_____

From

_____

Broadstreet Publishing™
Racine, WI 53403
Broadstreetpublishing.com

Bible Promises for Teens
© 2014 by Broadstreet Publishing

ISBN 978-1-4245-4902-3

The Holy Bible, New International Version®, NIV®. Copyright © 1973, 1978, 1984, 2011 by Biblica, Inc.® All rights reserved worldwide. The Holy Bible, New King James Version® (NKJV). Copyright © 1982 by Thomas Nelson, Inc. The New American Standard Bible® (NASB), copyright © 1960, 1962, 1963, 1968, 1971, 1972, 1973, 1975, 1977, 1995 by The Lockman Foundation. The New Revised Standard Version Bible (NRSV), Copyright © 1989 the Division of Christian Education of the National Council of the Churches of Christ in the United States of America. The Holy Bible, New Living Translation (NLT), copyright © 1996, 2004, 2007 by Tyndale House Foundation. Used by permission of Tyndale House Publishers, Inc., Carol Stream, Illinois 60188. *The Message* (MSG). Copyright © 1993, 1994, 1995, 1996, 2000, 2001, 2002. Used by permission of NavPress Publishing Group. *The Living Bible* (TLB) copyright © 1971 by Tyndale House Foundation. Used by permission of Tyndale House Publishers, Inc., Carol Stream, Illinois 60188. The New Century Version® (NCV). Copyright © 2005 by Thomas Nelson, Inc. Used by permission. All rights reserved.

Compiled by Barbara Farmer
Cover design by Josh Lewandowski
Interior design by James Baker | www.jamesbakerdesign.com

Printed in China

Contents

Alpha—God is the first place to go for all we need 6
Abandonment 8
Abuse 10
Acceptance 12

Addiction 16
Anger..18
Beauty 20
Blessings 22

Commitment..26
Contentment..28
Courage 30
Creativity..32

Depression 36
Discouragement...38
Encouragement 40
Enthusiasm...42

Eternity 46
Faith 48
Faithfulness 50
Family 52

Fear 56
Forgiveness...58
Friendship.. 60
Generosity..62

Goodness..66
Grace...68
Grief 70
Guidance 72

Guilt 76
Health 78
Helpfulness 80
Hope...82

Humility..86
Identity... 88
Inspiration 90
Integrity 92

Joy..96
Justice 98
Loneliness...100
Love..102

Money 106
Patience...108
Peace 110
Perseverance...112

Praise 116
Prayer...118
Promises..120
Purpose 122

Rebellion...126
Reconciliation...128
Respect..130
Salvation 132

Serving 136
Sexuality..138
Stress..140
Temptation 142

Thankfulness 146
Trust...148
Truth 150
Wisdom..152

Worry...156
Omega—God is the final answer for all we need.....................158

Alpha

GOD IS THE FIRST PLACE TO GO
FOR ALL THAT WE NEED

"I am the Alpha and the Omega, the Beginning
and the End," says the Lord, "who is and who was and
who is to come, the Almighty."

REVELATION 1:8 NKJV

I fall to my knees and pray to the Father,
the Creator of everything in heaven and on earth.
I pray that from his glorious, unlimited resources
he will empower you with inner strength through
his Spirit. Then Christ will make his home
in your hearts as you trust in him.

EPHESIANS 3:14–17 NLT

Jesus Christ is the same yesterday and today and forever.

HEBREWS 13:8 NASB

God is the one who provides seed for the farmer and then
bread to eat. In the same way, he will provide and
increase your resources and then produce
a great harvest of generosity in you.

2 CORINTHIANS 9:10 NLT

My God will supply all your needs according to His riches
in glory in Christ Jesus.

PHILIPPIANS 4:19 NASB

Abandonment

Who shall separate us from the love of Christ? Shall trouble
or hardship or persecution or famine or nakedness
or danger or sword?... No, in all these things we are
more than conquerors through him who loved us.
For I am convinced that neither death nor life, neither
angels nor demons, neither the present nor the future,
nor any powers, neither height nor depth, nor anything
else in all creation, will be able to separate us from
the love of God that is in Christ Jesus our Lord.

ROMANS 8:35–39 NIV

If my father and mother leave me,
the LORD will take me in.

PSALM 27:10 NCV

Be strong and courageous, do not be afraid...for the LORD
your God is the one who goes with you.
He will not fail you or forsake you.

DEUTERONOMY 31:6 NASB

GOD made my life complete when I placed all the
pieces before him.... GOD rewrote the text of my life when I
opened the book of my heart to his eyes.

PSALM 18:20, 24 MSG

My God is changeless in his love for me,
and he will come and help me.

PSALM 59:10 TLB

Abuse

Don't be afraid, I've redeemed you.
I've called your name. You're mine.
When you're in over your head, I'll be there with you.
When you're in rough waters, you will not go down.
When you're between a rock and a hard place,
it won't be a dead end—
Because I am God, your personal God,
The Holy of Israel, your Savior.
I paid a huge price for you...
That's how much you mean to me!
That's how much I love you!

ISAIAH 43:1–4 MSG

The Lord is close to the brokenhearted
and saves those who are crushed in spirit.

PSALM 34:18 NIV

You, O Lord, are a shield around me,
my glory, and the one who lifts up my head.

Psalm 3:3 nrsv

You are my refuge, a high tower where my enemies
can never reach me.

Psalm 61:3 tlb

My God in his steadfast love will meet me;
my God will let me look in triumph on my enemies.

Psalm 59:10 nrsv

The everlasting God is your place of safety,
and his arms will hold you up forever.

Deuteronomy 33:27 ncv

Acceptance

We have come to know and have believed the love
which God has for us. God is love, and the one who abides
in love abides in God, and God abides in him.
We love, because He first loved us.

1 JOHN 4:16, 19 NASB

Here I am! I stand at the door and knock. If anyone
hears my voice and opens the door, I will come in
and eat with that person, and they with me.

REVELATION 3:20 NIV

God is faithful, who has called you into fellowship
with his Son, Jesus Christ our Lord.

1 CORINTHIANS 1:9 NIV

How blessed is God!... Long before he
laid down earth's foundations, he had us in mind,
had settled on us as the focus of his love, to be made
whole and holy by his love. Long, long ago he decided
to adopt us into his family through Jesus Christ.
(What pleasure he took in planning this!) He wanted us
to enter into the celebration of his lavish gift-giving
by the hand of his beloved Son.

EPHESIANS 1:3–6 MSG

The Father gives me the people who are mine. Every one of
them will come to me, and I will always accept them.

JOHN 6:37 NCV

Addiction

Do you not know that your bodies are temples of the Holy
Spirit, who is in you, whom you have received from God?
You are not your own; you were bought at a price.
Therefore honor God with your bodies.

1 Corinthians 6:19–20 niv

My child, listen and be wise:
Keep your heart on the right course.
Do not carouse with drunkards
or feast with gluttons,
for they are on their way to poverty,
and too much sleep clothes them in rags.

Proverbs 23:19–21 nlt

You're blessed when you've worked up a good appetite for
God. He's food and drink in the best meal you'll ever eat.

Matthew 5:6 msg

Show me Your ways, O Lord;
Teach me Your paths.
Lead me in Your truth and teach me.

Psalm 25:4–5 NKJV

Now the Lord is the Spirit, and where
the Spirit of the Lord is, there is freedom.

2 Corinthians 3:17 NRSV

I will teach you wisdom's ways
and lead you in straight paths.
When you walk, you won't be held back;
when you run, you won't stumble.
Take hold of my instructions; don't let them go.
Guard them, for they are the key to life.

Proverbs 4:11–13 NLT

Anger

Always be willing to listen and slow to speak. Do not
become angry easily, because anger will not help you
live the right kind of life God wants.

JAMES 1:19–20 NCV

A gentle answer turns away wrath,
But a harsh word stirs up anger.

PROVERBS 15:1 NASB

Make sure it's all gone for good: bad temper, irritability,
meanness, profanity, dirty talk. Don't lie to one another.
You're done with that old life. It's like a filthy set of
ill-fitting clothes you've stripped off and put in the fire.
Now you're dressed in a new wardrobe.
Every item of your new way of life is custom-made
by the Creator, with his label on it.

COLOSSIANS 3:8–10 MSG

Get rid of all bitterness, rage, anger, harsh words,
and slander, as well as all types of evil behavior.
Instead, be kind to each other, tenderhearted, forgiving
one another, just as God through Christ has forgiven you.

EPHESIANS 4:31–32 NLT

People with understanding control their anger;
a hot temper shows great foolishness.

PROVERBS 14:29 NLT

Whatever is true, whatever is noble, whatever is right,
whatever is pure, whatever is lovely, whatever is
admirable—if anything is excellent or praiseworthy—
think about such things.

PHILIPPIANS 4:8 NIV

Beauty

Don't be concerned about the outward beauty of
fancy hairstyles, expensive jewelry, or beautiful clothes.
You should clothe yourselves instead with the beauty that
comes from within, the unfading beauty of a gentle and
quiet spirit, which is so precious to God.

1 PETER 3:3–4 NLT

You formed my inward parts;
You covered me in my mother's womb.
I will praise You,
for I am fearfully and wonderfully made;
Marvelous are Your works,
And that my soul knows very well.

PSALM 139:13–14 NKJV

The LORD does not look at the things people look at.
People look at the outward appearance,
but the LORD looks at the heart.

1 SAMUEL 16:7 NIV

Has anyone by fussing in front of the mirror ever gotten
taller by so much as an inch? All this time and money
wasted on fashion—do you think it makes that much
difference? Instead of looking at the fashions, walk out into
the fields and look at the wildflowers. They never primp or
shop, but have you ever seen color and design quite like it?
The ten best-dressed men and women in the country
look shabby alongside them.

MATTHEW 6:27–29 MSG

Blessings

You prepare a feast for me
in the presence of my enemies.
You honor me by anointing my head with oil.
My cup overflows with blessings.

PSALM 23:5 NLT

When you give a dinner or a supper, do not ask...
your relatives, nor rich neighbors, lest they also invite you
back, and you be repaid. But...invite the poor, the maimed,
the lame, the blind. And you will be blessed.

LUKE 14:12–14 NKJV

Oh, taste and see that the LORD is good;
Blessed is the man who trusts in Him!

PSALM 34:8 NKJV

The LORD bless you, and keep you;
The LORD make His face shine on you,
And be gracious to you;
The LORD lift up His countenance on you,
And give you peace.

NUMBERS 6:24–26 NASB

Do not repay evil with evil or insult with insult.
On the contrary, repay evil with blessing, because to this
you were called so that you may inherit a blessing.

1 PETER 3:9 NIV

GOD's blessing makes life rich;
nothing we do can improve on God.

PROVERBS 10:22 MSG

Commitment

Commit everything you do to the LORD.
Trust him, and he will help you.
He will make your innocence radiate like the dawn,
and the justice of your cause will shine like the noonday sun.

PSALM 37:5–6 NLT

Let the beauty of the LORD our God be upon us,
And establish the work of our hands for us;
Yes, establish the work of our hands.

PSALM 90:17 NKJV

Work willingly at whatever you do, as though you were
working for the Lord rather than for people.

COLOSSIANS 3:23 NLT

Confirm God's invitation to you, his choice of you.
Don't put it off; do it now. Do this, and you'll have
your life on a firm footing.

2 PETER 1:10–11 MSG

Commit your work to the Lord,
then it will succeed.

PROVERBS 16:3 TLB

I have fought the good fight, I have finished the race,
I have kept the faith. From now on there is reserved for me
the crown of righteousness, which the Lord, the righteous
judge, will give me on that day, and not only to me but also
to all who have longed for his appearing.

2 TIMOTHY 4:7–8 NRSV

Contentment

● ● ● ● ● ●

If God gives such attention to the appearance of
wildflowers—most of which are never even seen—
don't you think he'll attend to you, take pride in you,
do his best for you? What I'm trying to do here is to
get you to relax, to not be so preoccupied with *getting*,
so you can respond to God's *giving*. People who don't know
God and the way he works fuss over these things,
but you know both God and how he works. Steep your life
in God-reality, God-initiative, God-provisions.
Don't worry about missing out. You'll find
all your everyday human concerns will be met.

MATTHEW 6:30–33 MSG

I have learned how to be content with whatever I have.
I know how to live on almost nothing or with everything.
I have learned the secret of living in every situation,
whether it is with a full stomach or empty,
with plenty or little. For I can do everything through Christ,
who gives me strength.

PHILIPPIANS 4:11–13 NLT

You're blessed when you're content with just who you are—
no more, no less. That's the moment you find yourselves
proud owners of everything that can't be bought.

MATTHEW 5:5 MSG

Courage

Be strong in the Lord and in his mighty power.
Put on all of God's armor so that you will be able
to stand firm against all strategies of the devil.
For we are not fighting against flesh-and-blood enemies,
but against evil rulers and authorities of the unseen
world, against mighty powers in this dark world,
and against evil spirits in the heavenly places.
Therefore, put on every piece of God's armor so you
will be able to resist the enemy in the time of evil.
Then after the battle you will still be standing firm.
Stand your ground, putting on the belt of truth and the
body armor of God's righteousness. For shoes, put on
the peace that comes from the Good News so that you
will be fully prepared. In addition to all of these, hold up
the shield of faith to stop the fiery arrows of the devil.
Put on salvation as your helmet, and take the sword
of the Spirit, which is the word of God.

EPHESIANS 6:10–17 NLT

Be of good courage,
And He shall strengthen your heart,
All you who hope in the LORD.

The LORD will keep you from all harm—
he will watch over your life;
the LORD will watch over your coming and going
both now and forevermore.

May he give you the power to
accomplish all the good things
your faith prompts you to do.

Creativity

In his grace, God has given us different gifts for doing
certain things well. So if God has given you the ability to
prophesy, speak out with as much faith as God has given
you. If your gift is serving others, serve them well.
If you are a teacher, teach well. If your gift is to
encourage others, be encouraging. If it is giving,
give generously. If God has given you leadership ability,
take the responsibility seriously. And if you have a gift for
showing kindness to others, do it gladly.

ROMANS 12:6–8 NLT

Go after a life of love as if your life depended on it—
because it does. Give yourselves to the gifts God gives you.
Most of all, try to proclaim his truth.

1 CORINTHIANS 14:1 MSG

There are different kinds of gifts,
but the same Spirit distributes them. There are
different kinds of service, but the same Lord.
There are different kinds of working,
but in all of them and in everyone
it is the same God at work.

1 CORINTHIANS 12:4–6 NIV

For we are God's masterpiece.
He has created us anew in Christ Jesus,
so we can do the good things
he planned for us long ago.

EPHESIANS 2:10 NLT

Depression

I keep asking that the God of our Lord Jesus Christ,
the glorious Father, may give you the Spirit of wisdom
and revelation, so that you may know him better.
I pray that the eyes of your heart may be enlightened
in order that you may know the hope to which he
has called you, the riches of his glorious inheritance
in his holy people, and his incomparably
great power for us who believe.

EPHESIANS 1:17–19 NIV

I will give them a crown to replace their ashes,
and the oil of gladness to replace their sorrow,
and clothes of praise to replace their spirit of sadness.

ISAIAH 61:3 NCV

No eye has seen, no ear has heard, and no mind
has imagined what God has prepared
for those who love him.

1 CORINTHIANS 2:9 NLT

I am the Light of the world; he who follows Me will not
walk in the darkness, but will have the Light of life.

JOHN 8:12 NASB

Praise be to the God and Father of our Lord Jesus Christ,
the Father of compassion and the God of all comfort,
who comforts us in all our troubles, so that we can comfort
those in any trouble with the comfort
we ourselves receive from God.

2 CORINTHIANS 1:3–4 NIV

Discouragement

In all this you greatly rejoice, though now
for a little while you may have had to suffer grief
in all kinds of trials. These have come so that
the proven genuineness of your faith—of greater worth
than gold, which perishes even though refined by fire—
may result in praise, glory and honor
when Jesus Christ is revealed.

1 PETER 1:6–9 NIV

Do not lose the courage you had in the past, which has a
great reward. You must hold on, so you can do what God
wants and receive what he has promised.

HEBREWS 10:35–36 NCV

We are pressed on every side by troubles, but we are not
crushed. We are perplexed, but not driven to despair.
We are hunted down, but never abandoned by God.
We get knocked down, but we are not destroyed.

2 Corinthians 4:8–9 nlt

Let not your heart be troubled; you believe in God,
believe also in Me. In My Father's house are
many mansions.... I go to prepare a place for you.
And if I go and prepare a place for you,
I will come again and receive you to Myself;
that where I am, there you may be also.

John 14:1–3 nkjv

Encouragement

Let everything you say be good and helpful, so that your words will be an encouragement to those who hear them.

EPHESIANS 4:29 NLT

Remind the people...to be ready to do whatever is good,... to be peaceable and considerate, and always to be gentle toward everyone.

TITUS 3:1–2 NIV

Pleasant words are like a honeycomb, sweetness to the soul and health to the bones.

PROVERBS 16:24 NKJV

Encourage one another and build each other up, just as in fact you are doing.

1 THESSALONIANS 5:11 NIV

Those who hope in the LORD
will renew their strength.
They will soar on wings like eagles;
they will run and not grow weary,
they will walk and not be faint.

ISAIAH 40:31 NIV

You have been chosen by God himself—you are priests of
the King, you are holy and pure, you are God's very own—
all this so that you may show to others how God called you
out of the darkness into his wonderful light.

1 PETER 2:9 TLB

You, O LORD, are a shield around me,
my glory, and the one who lifts up my head.

PSALM 3:3 NRSV

Enthusiasm

Pay careful attention to your own work,
for then you will get the satisfaction
of a job well done, and you won't need to
compare yourself to anyone else. For we
are each responsible for our own conduct.

GALATIANS 6:4–5 NLT

Be wise in the way you act...;
make the most of every opportunity.
Let your conversation be always full of grace,
seasoned with salt, so that you
may know how to answer everyone.

COLOSSIANS 4:5–6 NIV

Work with enthusiasm, as though you were working for the Lord rather than for people. Remember that the Lord will reward each one of us for the good we do.

EPHESIANS 6:7–8 NLT

Dear friend, listen well to my words;
tune your ears to my voice.
Keep my message in plain view at all times.
Concentrate! Learn it by heart!
Those who discover these words live,
really live; body and soul....
Keep vigilant watch over your heart;
that's where life starts.

PROVERBS 4:20–23 MSG

Eternity

I'm asking GOD for one thing, only one thing:
To live with him in his house my whole life long.
I'll contemplate his beauty; I'll study at his feet.

PSALM 27:4 MSG

For our light and momentary troubles are achieving for us
an eternal glory that far outweighs them all. So we fix our
eyes not on what is seen, but on what is unseen. Since
what is seen is temporary, but what is unseen is eternal.

2 CORINTHIANS 4:17–18 NIV

Before the mountains were brought forth,
or ever you had formed the earth and the world,
from everlasting to everlasting you are God.

PSALM 90:2 NRSV

We are citizens of heaven, where the Lord Jesus Christ lives. And we are eagerly waiting for him to return as our Savior. He will take our weak mortal bodies and change them into glorious bodies like his own.

PHILIPPIANS 3:20–21 NLT

I will come back and take you to be with me that you also may be where I am.

JOHN 14:3 NIV

Surely goodness and mercy shall follow me
All the days of my life;
And I will dwell in the house of the LORD
Forever.

PSALM 23:6 NKJV

Faith

Faith is confidence in what we hope for
and assurance about what we do not see.

HEBREWS 11:1 NIV

By entering through faith into what God has always wanted
to do for us—set us right with him, make us fit for him—
we have it all together with God because of our
Master Jesus. And that's not all: We throw open our doors
to God and discover at the same moment that he has
already thrown open his door to us. We find ourselves
standing where we always hoped we might stand—
out in the wide open spaces of God's grace and glory,
standing tall and shouting our praise.

ROMANS 5:1–2 MSG

Without faith it is impossible to please God, because anyone who comes to him must believe that he exists and that he rewards those who earnestly seek him.

HEBREWS 11:6 NIV

As many as received Him, to them He gave the right to become children of God, even to those who believe in His name.

JOHN 1:12 NASB

Through Christ you have come to trust in God. And you have placed your faith and hope in God because he raised Christ from the dead and gave him great glory.

1 PETER 1:21 NLT

Faithfulness

● ● ● ● ● ●

You must remain faithful to the things you
have been taught. You know they are true, for you know
you can trust those who taught you. You have
been taught the holy Scriptures from childhood, and they
have given you the wisdom to receive the salvation
that comes by trusting in Christ Jesus.

2 TIMOTHY 3:14–15 NLT

The steadfast love of the LORD never ceases,
his mercies never come to an end;
they are new every morning;
great is your faithfulness.

LAMENTATIONS 3:22–23 NRSV

Your love, Lord, reaches to the heavens,
your faithfulness to the skies.
Your righteousness is like the highest mountains,
your justice like the great deep.
You, Lord, preserve both people and animals.
How priceless is your unfailing love, O God!
People take refuge in the shadow of your wings.
They feast on the abundance of your house;
you give them drink from your river of delights.
For with you is the fountain of life;
in your light we see light.

PSALM 36:5–9 NIV

Family

Brothers and sisters, we ask you to appreciate those who
work hard among you, who lead you in the Lord and teach
you. Respect them with a very special love because of the
work they do. Live in peace with each other....
Be patient with everyone. Be sure that no one pays back
wrong for wrong, but always try to do what is good
for each other and for all people.

1 THESSALONIANS 5:12–15 NCV

You're blessed when you can show people how to cooperate
instead of compete or fight. That's when you discover who
you really are, and your place in God's family.

MATTHEW 5:9 MSG

Obey your parents in the Lord, for this is right.
"Honor your father and mother"—which is
the first commandment with a promise—
"so that it may go well with you and that
you may enjoy long life on the earth."

EPHESIANS 6:1–3 NIV

The father of godly children has cause for joy.
What a pleasure to have children who are wise.
So give your father and mother joy!
May she who gave you birth be happy.

PROVERBS 23:24–25 NLT

Fear

Even though I walk through the valley of the shadow of death,
I fear no evil, for You are with me;
Your rod and Your staff, they comfort me.
You prepare a table before me in the presence of my enemies;
You have anointed my head with oil;
My cup overflows.

PSALM 23:4–5 NASB

Steep yourself in God-reality, God-initiative,
God-provisions. You'll find all your everyday human
concerns will be met. Don't be afraid of missing out.
You're my dearest friends! The Father wants to give you
the very kingdom itself.

LUKE 12:31–32 MSG

Love has been perfected among us in this:
that we may have boldness in the day of judgment;
because as He is, so are we in this world. There is
no fear in love; but perfect love casts out fear.

1 JOHN 4:17–18 NKJV

God has not given us a spirit of fear and timidity,
but of power, love, and self-discipline.

2 TIMOTHY 1:7 NLT

The LORD is my light and my salvation—
whom shall I fear?
The LORD is the stronghold of my life—
of whom shall I be afraid?

PSALM 27:1 NIV

Forgiveness

The LORD is compassionate and gracious,
slow to anger, abounding in love.
He will not always accuse,
nor will he harbor his anger forever;
he does not treat us as our sins deserve....
For as high as the heavens are above the earth,
so great is his love for those who fear him;
as far as the east is from the west,
so far has he removed our transgressions from us.

PSALM 103:8–12 NIV

If anyone is in Christ, he is a new creation; old things have
passed away; behold, all things have become new.

2 CORINTHIANS 5:17 NKJV

When you were stuck in your old sin-dead life,
you were incapable of responding to God. God brought you
alive—right along with Christ! Think of it! All sins forgiven,
the slate wiped clean, that old arrest warrant canceled
and nailed to Christ's cross.

COLOSSIANS 2:13 MSG

If we confess our sins, He is faithful and just to forgive us
our sins and to cleanse us from all unrighteousness.

1 JOHN 1:9 NKJV

Make allowance for each other's faults, and forgive anyone
who offends you. Remember, the Lord forgave you,
so you must forgive others.

COLOSSIANS 3:13 NLT

Friendship

There are "friends" who pretend to be friends,
but there is a friend who sticks closer than a brother.

PROVERBS 18:24 TLB

My command is this: Love each other as I have loved you.
Greater love has no one than this:
to lay down one's life for one's friends.

JOHN 15:12–13 NIV

The right word at the right time
is like a custom-made piece of jewelry,
And a wise friend's timely reprimand
is like a gold ring slipped on your finger.
Reliable friends who do what they say
are like cool drinks in sweltering heat—refreshing!

PROVERBS 25:12–13 MSG

Perfume and incense bring joy to the heart,
and the pleasantness of a friend
springs from their heartfelt advice.

PROVERBS 27:9 NIV

Two are better than one,
because they have a good return for their labor:
If either of them falls down,
one can help the other up.

ECCLESIASTES 4:9–10 NIV

The amazing grace of the Master, Jesus Christ,
the extravagant love of God, the intimate friendship
of the Holy Spirit, be with all of you.

2 CORINTHIANS 13:14 MSG

Generosity

Give, and it will be given to you.
A good measure, pressed down, shaken together
and running over, will be poured into your lap.
For with the measure you use,
it will be measured to you.

LUKE 6:38 NIV

One person gives freely, yet gains even more;
another withholds unduly, but comes to poverty.
A generous person will prosper;
whoever refreshes others will be refreshed.

PROVERBS 11:24–25 NIV

Remember this—a farmer who plants only a few seeds will get a small crop. But the one who plants generously will get a generous crop. You must each decide in your heart how much to give. And don't give reluctantly or in response to pressure. "For God loves a person who gives cheerfully." And God will generously provide all you need. Then you will always have everything you need and plenty left over to share with others.... Yes, you will be enriched in every way so that you can always be generous. And when we take your gifts to those who need them, they will thank God.

2 CORINTHIANS 9:6–8, 11 NLT

Goodness

Look at those who are honest and good,
for a wonderful future awaits those who love peace.

PSALM 37:37 NLT

He has told you...what is good;
And what does the LORD require of you
But to do justice, to love kindness,
And to walk humbly with your God?

MICAH 6:8 NASB

Let us not become weary in doing good, for at the proper
time we will reap a harvest if we do not give up. Therefore,
as we have opportunity, let us do good to all people.

GALATIANS 6:9–10 NIV

Make sure you don't take things for granted and go slack in working for the common good; share what you have with others. God takes particular pleasure in acts of worship... that take place in kitchen and workplace and on the streets.

HEBREWS 13:16 MSG

Always pursue what is good both for yourselves and for all. Rejoice always, pray without ceasing, in everything give thanks.... Test all things; hold fast what is good.

1 THESSALONIANS 5:15–18, 21 NKJV

Keep your eyes focused on what is right, and look straight ahead to what is good.

PROVERBS 4:25 NCV

Grace

We are made right with God by placing our faith in Jesus
Christ. And this is true for everyone who believes,
no matter who we are. For everyone has sinned;
we all fall short of God's glorious standard. Yet God,
with undeserved kindness, declares that we are righteous.
He did this through Christ Jesus when he freed us
from the penalty for our sins.

ROMANS 3:22–24 NLT

He has saved us and called us to a holy life—
not because of anything we have done but because of his
own purpose and grace.

2 TIMOTHY 1:9 NIV

Since we have a great High Priest who has entered heaven,
Jesus the Son of God, let us hold firmly to what we believe.
This High Priest of ours understands our weaknesses, for
he faced all of the same testings we do, yet he did not sin.
So let us come boldly to the throne of our gracious God.
There we will receive his mercy, and we will find grace
to help us when we need it most.

HEBREWS 4:14–16 NLT

By grace you have been saved through faith, and this is
not your own doing; it is the gift of God—not the result of
works, so that no one may boast.

EPHESIANS 2:8–9 NRSV

Grief

God is the Father who is full of mercy and all comfort.
He comforts us every time we have trouble.

2 Corinthians 1:3–4 ncv

Dear brothers and sisters, we want you to know what will
happen to the believers who have died so you will not
grieve like people who have no hope. For since we believe
that Jesus died and was raised to life again, we also believe
that when Jesus returns, God will bring back with him the
believers who have died.

1 Thessalonians 4:13–14 nlt

Jesus said to her, "I am the resurrection and the life.
He who believes in Me, though he may die, he shall live."

John 11:25 nkjv

Now is your time of grief,
but I will see you again and you will rejoice,
and no one will take away your joy.

JOHN 16:22 NIV

He will wipe every tear from their eyes, and there will be
no more death or sorrow or crying or pain.
All these things are gone forever.

REVELATION 21:4 NLT

You're blessed when you feel you've lost what is
most dear to you. Only then can you be embraced
by the One most dear to you.

MATTHEW 5:4 MSG

Guidance

Trust in the LORD with all your heart,
And lean not on your own understanding;
In all your ways acknowledge Him,
And He shall direct your paths.

PROVERBS 3:5–6 NKJV

I'll take the hand of those who don't know the way,
who can't see where they're going.
I'll be a personal guide to them,
directing them through unknown country.

ISAIAH 42:16 MSG

When we obey him,
every path he guides us on is fragrant
with his lovingkindness and his truth.

PSALM 25:10 TLB

The LORD directs the steps of the godly.
He delights in every detail of their lives.
Though they stumble, they will never fall,
for the LORD holds them by the hand.

PSALM 37:23–24 NLT

I will instruct you and teach you in the way you should go;
I will counsel you with my loving eye on you.

PSALM 32:8 NIV

When you turn to the right or when you turn to the left,
your ears shall hear a word behind you, saying,
"This is the way; walk in it."

ISAIAH 30:21 NRSV

Guilt

Dear brothers and sisters, we can boldly enter heaven's
Most Holy Place because of the blood of Jesus.
By his death, Jesus opened a new and life-giving
way through the curtain into the Most Holy Place.
And since we have a great High Priest who
rules over God's house, let us go right into the
presence of God with sincere hearts fully trusting him.
For our guilty consciences have been sprinkled with
Christ's blood to make us clean, and our bodies
have been washed with pure water.
Let us hold tightly without wavering to the hope
we affirm, for God can be trusted to keep his promise.

HEBREWS 10:19–23 NLT

There is now no condemnation for those
who are in Christ Jesus, because through Christ Jesus
the law of the Spirit who gives life has set you free
from the law of sin and death.

ROMANS 8:1–2 NIV

I, I am the One who erases all your sins, for my sake;
I will not remember your sins.

ISAIAH 43:25 NCV

God did not send his Son into the world to
condemn the world, but to save the world through him.
Whoever believes in him is not condemned.

JOHN 3:17–18 NIV

Health

Praise the LORD, my soul,
and forget not all his benefits—
who forgives all your sins
and heals all your diseases,
who redeems your life from the pit
and crowns you with love and compassion,
who satisfies your desires with good things
so that your youth is renewed like the eagle's.

PSALM 103:2–5 NIV

Beloved, I pray that all may go well with you
and that you may be in good health,
just as it is well with your soul.

3 JOHN 1:2 NRSV

Are you hurting? Pray. Do you feel great? Sing.
Are you sick? Call the church leaders together to pray
and anoint you with oil in the name of the Master.
Believing-prayer will heal you, and Jesus will put you on
your feet. And if you've sinned, you'll be forgiven—
healed inside and out.

JAMES 5:14–15 MSG

My child, pay attention to what I say.
Listen carefully to my words.
Don't lose sight of them.
Let them penetrate deep into your heart,
for they bring life to those who find them,
and healing to their whole body.

PROVERBS 4:20–22 NLT

Helpfulness

Are your hearts tender and compassionate?
Then make me truly happy by agreeing wholeheartedly
with each other, loving one another, and working together
with one mind and purpose.

PHILIPPIANS 2:1–2 NLT

God is not unjust; he will not forget your work and the love
you have shown him as you have helped his people and
continue to help them.

HEBREWS 6:10 NIV

Let us consider how we may spur one another on
toward love and good deeds.

HEBREWS 10:24 NIV

"Lord, when was it that we saw you hungry and gave you food, or thirsty and gave you something to drink? And when was it that we saw you a stranger and welcomed you, or naked and gave you clothing? And when was it that we saw you sick or in prison and visited you?" And the king will answer them, "Truly I tell you, just as you did it to one of the least of these who are members of my family, you did it to me."

MATTHEW 25:37–40 NRSV

Carry each other's burdens, and in this way you will fulfill the law of Christ.... Therefore, as we have opportunity, let us do good to all people.

GALATIANS 6:2, 10 NIV

Hope

May the God of hope fill you with all joy and peace as you trust in him, so that you may overflow with hope.

ROMANS 15:13 NIV

We can rejoice, too, when we run into problems and trials, for we know that they help us develop endurance. And endurance develops strength of character, and character strengthens our confident hope of salvation. And this hope will not lead to disappointment. For we know how dearly God loves us, because he has given us the Holy Spirit to fill our hearts with his love.

ROMANS 5:3–5 NLT

There is surely a future hope for you,
and your hope will not be cut off.

PROVERBS 23:18 NIV

In hope we have been saved, but hope that is seen
is not hope; for who hopes for what he already sees?
But if we hope for what we do not see,
with perseverance we wait eagerly for it.

Romans 8:24–25 nasb

The Lord is good to those whose hope is in him,
to the one who seeks him.

Lamentations 3:25 niv

God...rekindles burned-out lives with fresh hope,
Restoring dignity and respect to their lives—
a place in the sun!

1 Samuel 2:7–8 msg

Humility

Where you have envy and selfish ambition, there you find disorder and every evil practice. But the wisdom that comes from heaven is first of all pure; then peace-loving, considerate, submissive, full of mercy and good fruit, impartial and sincere. Peacemakers who sow in peace reap a harvest of righteousness.

JAMES 3:16–18 NIV

Those who accept correction gain understanding. Respect for the LORD will teach you wisdom. If you want to be honored, you must be humble.

PROVERBS 15:32–33 NCV

Humble yourselves in the sight of the Lord, and He will lift you up.

JAMES 4:10 NKJV

In your relationships with one another,
have the same mindset as Christ Jesus:
Who, being in very nature God,
did not consider equality with God something
to be used to his own advantage;
rather, he made himself nothing
by taking the very nature of a servant,
being made in human likeness.
And being found in appearance as a man,
he humbled himself
by becoming obedient to death—
even death on a cross!
Therefore God exalted him to the highest place
and gave him the name that is above every name.

PHILIPPIANS 2:5–9 NIV

Identity

Take your everyday, ordinary life—your sleeping, eating,
going-to-work, and walking-around life—and place it
before God as an offering. Embracing what God does for
you is the best thing you can do for him. Don't become so
well-adjusted to your culture that you fit into it without
even thinking. Instead, fix your attention on God.
You'll be changed from the inside out. Readily recognize
what he wants from you, and quickly respond to it.
Unlike the culture around you, always dragging you down
to its level of immaturity, God brings the best out of you,
develops well-formed maturity in you.

ROMANS 12:1–2 MSG

See what great love the Father has lavished on us,
that we should be called children of God!
And that is what we are!

1 JOHN 3:1 NIV

You did not receive a spirit of slavery
to fall back into fear, but you have received
a spirit of adoption. When we cry, "Abba! Father!"
it is that very Spirit bearing witness with
our spirit that we are children of God.

ROMANS 8:15–16 NRSV

Do everything without grumbling or arguing,
so that you may become blameless and pure,
"children of God without fault in a warped
and crooked generation." Then you will
shine among them like stars in the sky
as you hold firmly to the word of life.

PHILIPPIANS 2:14–16 NIV

Inspiration

I'm not saying that I have this all together, that I have it
made. But I am well on my way, reaching out for Christ,
who has so wondrously reached out for me.

PHILIPPIANS 3:12 MSG

Since we are surrounded by such a huge crowd of witnesses
to the life of faith, let us strip off every weight that
slows us down.... And let us run with endurance
the race God has set before us.

HEBREWS 12:1 NLT

I have come that they may have life, and that they may
have it more abundantly.

JOHN 10:10 NKJV

You are the light of the world. A town built on a hill cannot be hidden. Neither do people light a lamp and put it under a bowl. Instead they put it on its stand, and it gives light to everyone in the house. In the same way, let your light shine before others, that they may see your good deeds and glorify your Father in heaven.

MATTHEW 5:14–16 NIV

Pursue a righteous life—a life of wonder, faith, love, steadiness, courtesy. Run hard and fast in the faith. Seize the eternal life, the life you were called to, the life you so fervently embraced in the presence of so many witnesses.

1 TIMOTHY 6:11–12 MSG

Integrity

Don't let anyone look down on you because you are young,
but set an example for the believers in speech,
in conduct, in love, in faith and in purity.

1 Timothy 4:12 niv

The Lord grants wisdom!
From his mouth come knowledge and understanding.
He grants a treasure of common sense to the honest.
He is a shield to those who walk with integrity.

Proverbs 2:6–7 nlt

A good name is to be chosen rather than great riches,
Loving favor rather than silver and gold.

Proverbs 22:1 nkjv

The Lord detests lying lips,
but he delights in people who are trustworthy.

Proverbs 12:22 niv

The highway of the upright avoids evil;
those who guard their ways preserve their lives.

PROVERBS 16:17 NIV

Plant your seed in the morning and keep busy
all afternoon, for you don't know if profit will come from
one activity or another—or maybe both.

ECCLESIASTES 11:6 NLT

Love and truth form a good leader;
sound leadership is founded on loving integrity.

PROVERBS 20:28 MSG

Whoever pursues righteousness and love finds life,
prosperity and honor.

PROVERBS 21:21 NIV

Joy

He will yet fill your mouth with laughter
and your lips with shouts of joy.

JOB 8:21 NIV

This is the day the LORD has made;
We will rejoice and be glad in it.

PSALM 118:24 NKJV

Be truly glad. There is wonderful joy ahead....
You love him even though you have never seen him.
Though you do not see him now, you trust him; and you
rejoice with a glorious, inexpressible joy.

1 PETER 1:6, 8 NLT

May the God of hope fill you with all joy
and peace in believing.

ROMANS 15:13 NKJV

You shall go out in joy,
and be led back in peace;
the mountains and the hills before you
shall burst into song,
and all the trees of the field shall clap their hands.

Isaiah 55:12 nrsv

Let all those rejoice who put their trust in You;
Let them ever shout for joy, because You defend them;
Let those also who love Your name
Be joyful in You.

Psalm 5:11 nkjv

The Lord has done great things for us,
and we are filled with joy.

Psalm 126:3 niv

Justice

Whoever pursues righteousness and love
finds life, prosperity and honor.

PROVERBS 21:21 NIV

He will not judge by appearance, false evidence,
or hearsay, but will defend the poor and the exploited.
He will rule against the wicked who oppress them.
For he will be clothed with fairness and with truth.

ISAIAH 11:3–5 TLB

The LORD secures justice for the poor
and upholds the cause of the needy.

PSALM 140:12 NIV

The righteous care about justice for the poor.

PROVERBS 29:7 NIV

The world is unprincipled. It's dog-eat-dog out there!
The world doesn't fight fair. But we don't live or
fight our battles that way—never have and never will.
The tools of our trade aren't for marketing or
manipulation, but they are for demolishing that
entire massively corrupt culture. We use our powerful
God-tools for smashing warped philosophies,
tearing down barriers erected against the
truth of God, fitting every loose thought and
emotion and impulse into the structure of life
shaped by Christ. Our tools are ready at hand for
clearing the ground of every obstruction and
building lives of obedience into maturity.

2 CORINTHIANS 10:3–6 MSG

Loneliness

O LORD, You have searched me and known me.
You know my sitting down and my rising up;
You understand my thought afar off.
You comprehend my path and my lying down,
And are acquainted with all my ways.
For there is not a word on my tongue,
But behold, O LORD, You know it altogether.

PSALM 139:1–4 NKJV

You will search again for the LORD your God.
And if you search for him with all your heart and soul,
you will find him.

DEUTERONOMY 4:29 NLT

I will not leave you as orphans; I will come to you.

JOHN 14:18 NIV

"Though the mountains be shaken
and the hills be removed,
yet my unfailing love for you will not be shaken
nor my covenant of peace be removed,"
says the LORD, who has compassion on you.

ISAIAH 54:10 NIV

The LORD is near to all who call on him,
to all who call on him in truth.

PSALM 145:18 NIV

By this we know that we abide in Him and He in us,
because He has given us of His Spirit.

1 JOHN 4:13 NASB

Remember, I am with you always, to the end of the age.

MATTHEW 28:20 NRSV

Love

If I speak in the tongues of men or of angels,
but do not have love, I am only a resounding gong or a
clanging cymbal. If I have the gift of prophecy and can
fathom all mysteries and all knowledge, and if I have a
faith that can move mountains, but do not have love,
I am nothing. If I give all I possess to the poor and give
over my body to hardship that I may boast,
but do not have love, I gain nothing.
Love is patient, love is kind. It does not envy,
it does not boast, it is not proud. It does not dishonor
others, it is not self-seeking, it is not easily angered,
it keeps no record of wrongs. Love does not delight in evil
but rejoices with the truth. It always protects,
always trusts, always hopes, always perseveres.
Love never fails.

1 CORINTHIANS 13:1–8 NIV

God showed how much he loved us by sending his one and
only Son into the world so that we might have eternal life
through him. This is real love—not that we loved God,
but that he loved us and sent his Son as a sacrifice to take
away our sins. Dear friends, since God loved us that much,
we surely ought to love each other. No one has ever seen
God. But if we love each other, God lives in us,
and his love is brought to full expression in us.

1 JOHN 4:9–12 NLT

Take nothing for granted. Stay wide-awake in prayer.
Most of all, love each other as if your life depended on it.
Love makes up for practically anything.

1 PETER 4:7–8 MSG

Money

Wealth from get-rich-quick schemes quickly disappears;
wealth from hard work grows over time.

PROVERBS 13:11 NLT

The one who sows sparingly will also reap sparingly,
and the one who sows bountifully will also reap
bountifully. Each of you must give as you have
made up your mind, not reluctantly or under
compulsion, for God loves a cheerful giver.
And God is able to provide you with every blessing in
abundance, so that by always having enough of everything,
you may share abundantly in every good work.

2 CORINTHIANS 9:6–8 NRSV

What good will it be for someone to gain the whole world,
yet forfeit their soul?

MATTHEW 16:26 NIV

Teach those who are rich in this world not to be proud and
not to trust in their money, which is so unreliable.
Their trust should be in God, who richly gives us all we
need for our enjoyment. Tell them to use their money
to do good. They should be rich in good works
and generous to those in need, always being ready
to share with others. By doing this they will be storing up
their treasure as a good foundation for the future so that
they may experience true life.

1 TIMOTHY 6:17–19 NLT

Patience

As those who have been chosen of God, holy and beloved,
put on a heart of compassion, kindness, humility,
gentleness and patience.... Beyond all these things
put on love, which is the perfect bond of unity.

COLOSSIANS 3:12, 14 NASB

God is pleased with you when you do what you know is
right and patiently endure unfair treatment.

1 PETER 2:19 NLT

I appeal to you, brothers and sisters, in the name of our
Lord Jesus Christ, that all of you agree with one another in
what you say and that there be no divisions among you,
but that you be perfectly united in mind and thought.

1 CORINTHIANS 1:10 NIV

Wait patiently for the LORD.
Be brave and courageous.
Yes, wait patiently for the LORD.

PSALM 27:14 NLT

Be patient, then, brothers and sisters, until the Lord's coming. See how the farmer waits for the land to yield its valuable crop, patiently waiting for the autumn and spring rains. You too, be patient and stand firm.

JAMES 5:7–8 NIV

May the Lord lead your hearts into a full understanding and expression of the love of God and the patient endurance that comes from Christ.

2 THESSALONIANS 3:5 NLT

Peace

Since we have been made right in God's sight by faith,
we have peace with God because of what Jesus Christ
our Lord has done for us. Because of our faith,
Christ has brought us into this place of undeserved
privilege where we now stand, and we confidently
and joyfully look forward to sharing God's glory.

ROMANS 5:1–2 NLT

These things I have spoken to you, so that in Me
you may have peace. In the world you have tribulation,
but take courage; I have overcome the world.

JOHN 16:33 NASB

God is not the author of confusion but of peace.

1 CORINTHIANS 14:33 NKJV

Do not be anxious about anything, but in every situation, by prayer and petition, with thanksgiving, present your requests to God. And the peace of God, which transcends all understanding, will guard your hearts and your minds in Christ Jesus.

PHILIPPIANS 4:6–7 NIV

If people's thinking is controlled by the sinful self, there is death. But if their thinking is controlled by the Spirit, there is life and peace.

ROMANS 8:6 NCV

Blessed are the peacemakers, for they will be called children of God.

MATTHEW 5:9 NIV

Perseverance

Dear brothers and sisters, I have not achieved it,
but I focus on this one thing: Forgetting the past
and looking forward to what lies ahead,
I press on to reach the end of the race and
receive the heavenly prize for which God,
through Christ Jesus, is calling us.

PHILIPPIANS 3:13–14 NLT

Consider it pure joy...whenever you face trials
of many kinds, because you know that the testing of your
faith produces perseverance. Let perseverance finish
its work so that you may be mature and complete,
not lacking anything.

JAMES 1:2–4 NIV

Blessed is the one who perseveres under trial because,
having stood the test, that person will receive the crown of
life that the Lord has promised to those who love him.

JAMES 1:12 NIV

I waited patiently for the LORD;
he turned to me and heard my cry.
He lifted me out of the slimy pit,
out of the mud and mire;
he set my feet on a rock
and gave me a firm place to stand.
He put a new song in my mouth,
a hymn of praise to our God.
Many will see and fear the LORD
and put their trust in him.

PSALM 40:1–3 NIV

Praise

Because your love is better than life,
my lips will glorify you.
I will praise you as long as I live,
and in your name I will lift up my hands.
I will be fully satisfied as with the richest of foods;
with singing lips my mouth will praise you.

PSALM 63:3–5 NIV

It's who you are and the way you live that count before
God. Your worship must engage your spirit in the pursuit
of truth. That's the kind of people the Father is out looking
for: those who are simply and honestly *themselves* before
him in their worship. God is sheer being itself—Spirit.
Those who worship him must do it out of their very being,
their spirits, their true selves, in adoration.

JOHN 4:23–24 MSG

Sing to the LORD a new song;
sing to the LORD, all the earth.
Sing to the LORD, praise his name;
proclaim his salvation day after day.
For great is the LORD and most worthy of praise.

PSALM 96:1–2, 4 NIV

By Him let us continually offer the sacrifice of praise to
God, that is, the fruit of our lips, giving thanks to His name.

HEBREWS 13:15 NKJV

I will praise you forever, O God,
for what you have done.
I will trust in your good name
in the presence of your faithful people.

PSALM 52:9 NLT

Prayer

Ask and it will be given to you; seek and you will find; knock and the door will be opened to you. For everyone who asks receives; the one who seeks finds; and to the one who knocks, the door will be opened.

MATTHEW 7:7–8 NIV

Love your enemies! Pray for those who persecute you! In that way, you will be acting as true children of your Father in heaven.

MATTHEW 5:44–45 NLT

I call on you, My God, for you will answer me; give ear to me and hear my prayer.

PSALM 17:6 NIV

The Spirit helps us in our weakness. We do not know what we ought to pray for, but the Spirit himself intercedes for us through wordless groans. And he who searches our hearts knows the mind of the Spirit, because the Spirit intercedes for God's people in accordance with the will of God.

ROMANS 8:26–27 NIV

I urge you, first of all, to pray for all people. Ask God to help them; intercede on their behalf, and give thanks for them. Pray this way for kings and all who are in authority so that we can live peaceful and quiet lives marked by godliness and dignity. This is good and pleases God our Savior, who wants everyone to be saved and to understand the truth.

1 TIMOTHY 2:1–4 NLT

Promises

Every good and perfect gift is from above, coming down
from the Father of the heavenly lights, who does not
change like shifting shadows.

JAMES 1:17 NIV

I am the vine; you are the branches. Those who remain
in me, and I in them, will produce much fruit.
For apart from me you can do nothing.... But if you remain
in me and my words remain in you, you may ask for
anything you want, and it will be granted!

JOHN 15:5, 7 NLT

All of God's promises have been fulfilled
in Christ with a resounding "Yes!"

2 CORINTHIANS 1:20 NLT

Not one word of all the good words which the LORD
your God spoke concerning you has failed;
all have been fulfilled for you.

JOSHUA 23:14 NASB

"For I know the plans I have for you," declares the LORD,
"plans to prosper you and not to harm you,
plans to give you hope and a future."

JEREMIAH 29:11 NIV

To him who is able to do immeasurably more than all
we ask or imagine, according to his power that is at work
within us, to him be glory...for ever and ever! Amen.

EPHESIANS 3:20–21 NIV

Purpose

What happens when we live God's way? He brings gifts into our lives...things like affection for others, exuberance about life..., a sense of compassion in the heart, and a conviction that a basic holiness permeates things and people.

GALATIANS 5:22–23 MSG

You make known to me the path of life;
you will fill me with joy in your presence.

PSALM 16:11 NIV

We know that all things work together for good to those who love God, to those who are the called according to His purpose.

ROMANS 8:28 NKJV

It's in Christ that we find out who we are and what we are living for. Long before we first heard of Christ and got our hopes up, he had his eye on us, had designs on us for glorious living, part of the overall purpose he is working out in everything and everyone.

EPHESIANS 1:11–12 MSG

Don't you realize that in a race everyone runs, but only one person gets the prize? So run to win! All athletes are disciplined in their training. They do it to win a prize that will fade away, but we do it for an eternal prize. So I run with purpose in every step.

1 CORINTHIANS 9:24–26 NLT

Rebellion

Because we belong to the day, we must live decent lives for all to see. Don't participate in the darkness of wild parties and drunkenness, or in sexual promiscuity and immoral living, or in quarreling and jealousy. Instead, clothe yourself with the presence of the Lord.

ROMANS 13:13–14 NLT

I am the LORD your God,
who teaches you what is best for you,
who directs you in the way you should go.
If only you had paid attention to my commands,
your peace would have been like a river,
your well-being like the waves of the sea.

ISAIAH 48:17–18 NIV

Once you were darkness, but now in the Lord you are light.
Live as children of light—for the fruit of the light is found
in all that is good and right and true.

EPHESIANS 5:8–9 NRSV

Keep your father's command
and do not forsake your mother's teaching.
Bind them always on your heart;
fasten them around your neck.
When you walk, they will guide you;
when you sleep, they will watch over you;
when you awake, they will speak to you.
For this command is a lamp,
this teaching is a light,
and correction and instruction
are the way to life.

PROVERBS 6:20–23 NIV

Reconciliation

● ● ● ● ● ●

We have stopped evaluating others from a human point
of view. At one time we thought of Christ merely from a
human point of view. How differently we know him now!
This means that anyone who belongs to Christ has become
a new person. The old life is gone; a new life has begun!
And all of this is a gift from God, who brought us back
to himself through Christ. And God has given us
this task of reconciling people to him.

2 CORINTHIANS 5:16–18 NLT

You were separate from Christ...foreigners to the covenants
of the promise, without hope and without God in the world.
But now in Christ Jesus you who once were far away
have been brought near.

EPHESIANS 2:12–13 NIV

God put the world square with himself through
the Messiah, giving the world a fresh start by
offering forgiveness of sins. God has given us
the task of telling everyone what he is doing.
We're Christ's representatives. God uses us
to persuade men and women to drop their
differences and enter into God's work of
making things right between them.
We're speaking for Christ himself now:
Become friends with God;
he's already a friend with you.

2 CORINTHIANS 5:19–20 MSG

Respect

Appreciate those who diligently labor among you, and have charge over you in the Lord and give you instruction... esteem them very highly in love because of their work. Live in peace with one another.

1 THESSALONIANS 5:12–13 NASB

Live as free people, but do not use your freedom as an excuse to do evil. Live as servants of God. Show respect for all people.

1 PETER 2:16–17 NCV

Get the word out. Teach all these things.... Immerse yourself in them. The people will all see you mature right before their eyes! Keep a firm grasp on both your character and your teaching.

1 TIMOTHY 4:11, 15–16 MSG

Never let loyalty and kindness leave you!
Tie them around your neck as a reminder.
Write them deep within your heart.
Then you will find favor with both God and people,
and you will earn a good reputation.

PROVERBS 3:3–4 NLT

Have confidence in your leaders and submit
to their authority, because they keep watch over you as
those who must give an account. Do this so that
their work will be a joy, not a burden,
for that would be of no benefit to you.

HEBREWS 13:17 NIV

Salvation

● ● ● ● ● ●

Once you were dead because of your disobedience and your
many sins.... All of us used to live that way, following the
passionate desires and inclinations of our sinful nature.
By our very nature we were subject to God's anger,
just like everyone else. But God is so rich in mercy,
and he loved us so much, that even though we were dead
because of our sins, he gave us life when he
raised Christ from the dead.

EPHESIANS 2:1, 3–5 NLT

If you declare with your mouth, "Jesus is Lord,"
and believe in your heart that God raised him
from the dead, you will be saved.

ROMANS 10:9 NIV

What a God we have! And how fortunate we are to have him, this Father of our Master Jesus! Because Jesus was raised from the dead, we've been given a brand-new life and have everything to live for, including a future in heaven—and the future starts now! God is keeping careful watch over us and the future. The Day is coming when you'll have it all—life healed and whole.

1 PETER 1:3–5 MSG

For God so loved the world that he gave his one and only Son, that whoever believes in him shall not perish but have eternal life.

JOHN 3:16 NIV

Serving

Each of you should use whatever gift you have received to serve others, as faithful stewards of God's grace in its various forms. If anyone serves, they should do so with the strength God provides, so that in all things God may be praised.

1 Peter 4:10–11 niv

Do you want to stand out? Then step down. Be a servant. If you puff yourself up, you'll get the wind knocked out of you. But if you're content to simply be yourself, your life will count for plenty.

Matthew 23:11–12 msg

Even the Son of Man came not to be served but to serve others and to give his life as a ransom for many.

Mark 10:45 nlt

He who is greatest among you, let him be as the
younger, and he who governs as he who serves.
For who is greater, he who sits at the table,
or he who serves? Is it not he who sits at the table?
Yet I am among you as the One who serves.

LUKE 22:26–27 NKJV

You have been called to live in freedom,
my brothers and sisters. But don't use your freedom
to satisfy your sinful nature. Instead, use your freedom
to serve one another in love.

GALATIANS 5:13 NLT

Sexuality

This is my prayer: that your love will flourish
and that you will not only love much but well.
Learn to love appropriately. You need to
use your head and test your feelings
so that your love is sincere and intelligent,
not sentimental gush.

PHILIPPIANS 1:9–10 MSG

You say, "I am allowed to do anything"—
but not everything is good for you.
And even though "I am allowed to do anything,"
I must not become a slave to anything.

1 CORINTHIANS 6:12 NLT

How can a young person stay on the path of purity?
By living according to your word.

PSALM 119:9 NIV

There's more to sex than mere skin on skin. Sex is as much
spiritual mystery as physical fact. As written in Scripture,
"The two become one." Since we want to become spiritually
one with the Master, we must not pursue the kind of sex
that avoids commitment and intimacy, leaving us more
lonely than ever—the kind of sex that can never "become
one."... In sexual sin we violate the sacredness of our own
bodies, these bodies that were made for God-given and
God-modeled love, for "becoming one" with another.

1 CORINTHIANS 6:16–18 MSG

Stress

Give your entire attention to what God is doing
right now, and don't get worked up about what may
or may not happen tomorrow. God will help you deal with
whatever hard things come up when the time comes.

Matthew 6:34 msg

Be glad for all God is planning for you.
Be patient in trouble, and prayerful always.

Romans 12:12 tlb

You're blessed when you're at the end of your rope.
With less of you there is more of God and his rule.

Matthew 5:3 msg

May the God who gives endurance and encouragement
give you the same attitude of mind toward each other
that Christ Jesus had.

ROMANS 15:5 NIV

Blessed is the one who trusts in the LORD,
whose confidence is in him.
They will be like a tree planted by the water
that sends out its roots by the stream.
It does not fear when heat comes;
its leaves are always green.
It has no worries in a year of drought
and never fails to bear fruit.

JEREMIAH 17:7–8 NIV

Temptation

If you think you are standing strong, be careful not to fall.
The temptations in your life are no different from what
others experience. And God is faithful. He will not
allow the temptation to be more than you can stand.
When you are tempted, he will show you a way out
so that you can endure.

1 CORINTHIANS 10:12–13 NLT

May God himself, the God of peace, sanctify you through
and through. May your whole spirit, soul and body be
kept blameless at the coming of our Lord Jesus Christ.
The one who calls you is faithful, and he will do it.

1 THESSALONIANS 5:23–24 NIV

I want you woven into a tapestry of love, in touch with everything there is to know of God. Then you will have minds confident and at rest, focused on Christ, God's great mystery. All the richest treasures of wisdom and knowledge are embedded in that mystery and nowhere else. And we've been shown the mystery! I'm telling you this because I don't want anyone leading you off on some wild-goose chase, after other so-called mysteries, or "the Secret."

COLOSSIANS 2:2–4 MSG

Thankfulness

Give thanks to the LORD, for he is good.
His love endures forever.

PSALM 136:1 NIV

Both riches and honor come from You,
And You reign over all.
In Your hand is power and might;
In Your hand it is to make great
And to give strength to all.
Now therefore, our God,
We thank You
And praise Your glorious name.

1 CHRONICLES 29:12–13 NKJV

Thanks be to God for his indescribable gift!

2 CORINTHIANS 9:15 NIV

Don't be drunk with wine, because that will ruin your life.
Instead, be filled with the Holy Spirit, singing psalms
and hymns and spiritual songs among yourselves,
and making music to the Lord in your hearts.
And give thanks for everything to God the Father
in the name of our Lord Jesus Christ.

EPHESIANS 5:18–20 NLT

We give thanks to God always for you, making mention of
you in our prayers; constantly bearing in mind your work
of faith and labor of love and steadfastness of hope.

1 THESSALONIANS 1:2–3 NASB

May you be filled with joy, always thanking the Father.
He has enabled you to share in the inheritance that
belongs to his people, who live in the light.

COLOSSIANS 1:11–12 NLT

Trust

● ● ● ● ● ●

I fall to my knees and pray to the Father,
the Creator of everything in heaven and on earth.
I pray that from his glorious, unlimited resources
he will empower you with inner strength through
his Spirit. Then Christ will make his home
in your hearts as you trust in him. Your roots
will grow down into God's love and keep you strong.
And may you have the power to understand,
as all God's people should, how wide, how long,
how high, and how deep his love is.
May you experience the love of Christ,
though it is too great to understand fully.
Then you will be made complete with all the
fullness of life and power that comes from God.

EPHESIANS 3:14–19 NLT

To you O LORD, I lift up my soul.
O my God, in you I trust.

PSALM 25:1–2 NRSV

The LORD is my strength and my shield;
My heart trusts in Him, and I am helped;
Therefore my heart exults,
And with my song I shall thank Him.

PSALM 28:7 NASB

You will keep him in perfect peace,
Whose mind is stayed on You,
Because he trusts in You.

ISAIAH 26:3 NKJV

Truth

Jesus said to him, "I am the way, the truth, and the life.
No one comes to the Father except through Me."

JOHN 14:6 NKJV

Teach me your ways, O LORD,
that I may live according to your truth!
Grant me purity of heart,
so that I may honor you.

PSALM 86:11 NLT

Jesus said, "If you hold to my teaching, you are really
my disciples. Then you will know the truth,
and the truth will set you free."

JOHN 8:31–32 NIV

Truthful words stand the test of time,
but lies are soon exposed.

PROVERBS 12:19 NLT

Everyone who does evil hates the light, and will not come into the light for fear that their deeds will be exposed. But whoever lives by the truth comes into the light, so that it may be seen plainly that what they have done has been done in the sight of God.

JOHN 3:20–21 NIV

Send out your light and your truth;
let them lead me;
let them bring me to your holy hill
and to your dwelling.

PSALM 43:3 NRSV

Open my eyes to see
the wonderful truths in your instructions.

PSALM 119:18 NLT

Wisdom

A wise man will hear and increase learning,
and a man of understanding will attain wise counsel.

PROVERBS 1:5 NKJV

Pay close attention, friend, to what your father tells you;
never forget what you learned at your mother's knee.
Wear their counsel like flowers in your hair,
like rings on your fingers.

PROVERBS 1:8–9 MSG

Wise words bring many benefits,
and hard work brings rewards.

PROVERBS 12:14 NLT

Wise men and women are always learning,
always listening for fresh insights.

PROVERBS 18:15 MSG

Cease listening to instruction...
And you will stray from the words of knowledge.

PROVERBS 19:27 NKJV

My child, never forget the things I have taught you.
Store my commands in your heart.
If you do this, you will live many years,
and your life will be satisfying.

PROVERBS 3:1–2 NLT

Teach the wise, and they will become even wiser;
teach good people, and they will learn even more.

PROVERBS 9:9 NCV

Wisdom is like honey for you:
if you find it, there is a future hope for you,
and your hope will not be cut off.

PROVERBS 24:14 NIV

Worry

Give all your worries and cares to God,
for he cares about you.

1 PETER 5:7 NLT

Do not worry about your life, what you will eat or drink;
or about your body, what you will wear. Is not life
more than food, and the body more than clothes?
Look at the birds of the air; they do not sow or reap or store
away in barns, and yet your heavenly Father feeds them.
Are you not much more valuable than they? Can any one
of you by worrying add a single hour to your life?

MATTHEW 6:25–27 NIV

Those who live in the shelter of the Most High
will find rest in the shadow of the Almighty....
Do not be afraid of the terrors of the night,
nor the arrow that flies in the day.
Do not dread the disease that stalks in darkness,
nor the disaster that strikes at midday....
If you make the LORD your refuge,
if you make the Most High your shelter,
no evil will conquer you;
no plague will come near your home.
For he will order his angels
to protect you wherever you go.

PSALM 91:1, 5–6, 9–11 NLT

Omega

GOD IS THE FINAL ANSWER
FOR ALL THAT WE NEED

Jesus stood and said…"Let anyone
who is thirsty come to me and drink.
Whoever believes in me, as Scripture
has said, rivers of living water will
flow from within them."

JOHN 7:37–38 NIV

Jesus…said, "For mortals it is
impossible, but not for God; for God
all things are possible."

MARK 10:27 NRSV

God can do anything, you know—
far more than you could ever imagine
or guess or request in your wildest dreams!

Ephesians 3:20 msg

I am the Alpha and the Omega—
the Beginning and the End.
To all who are thirsty I will give freely
from the springs of the water of life.

Revelation 21:6 nlt